# GREEN SOCIETIES

Five Nordic States as Leaders in Conservation

CHRISTINE INGEBRITSEN

NEWMAN SPRINGS PUBLISHING
320 Broad Street
Red Bank, NJ 07701

First originally published by Newman Springs Publishing 2024

ISBN 979-8-89061-235-9 (Paperback)
ISBN 979-8-89061-236-6 (Digital)

Printed in the United States of America

# Scandinavia

# Preface

## *What Are Green Societies?*

This study focuses on the five Nordic states who are ahead of others and where they have been preparing for the future. Denmark, Finland, Iceland, Norway, and Sweden are limiting scarce resources. And conservation is uniquely on the policy making of the green societies in this corner of Europe.

As capitalism changes, so too must our relationship with nature. There are even more reasons to restrain from overusing common resources. In the political agendas of these states, and their societal norms, we are not only forward-looking; they have already arrived.

Scandinavia's five green societies (Denmark, Sweden, Norway, Iceland, and Finland) are among a group of references that include *Hygge*, *Lagom*, and *Swedish Death Cleaning*.

Green societies are distinct polities in Scandinavia and are exceptional ways in this corner of Europe: a role model of taming capitalism.

How do green societies differ from *sustainability*? In the report, *Our Common Future* stated, "development that meets the needs of the present without compromising the ability of future generations to meet their own needs." The green societies are exceptional, by developing distinct economic policies and are already leaders in the conservation of vital resources.

The focus on the five Scandinavian societies is uniquely diverse and forward-looking. The green societies of Scandinavia are the focus of this study, embedded in a region of ecoinnovation, and are leaders pursuing conservation in the North.

# Introduction

Prominent scholars and policymakers from Scandinavia have distinct views about the role of ecology and capitalism. The Norwegian naturalist Arne Naess made convincing arguments against capitalism and promoted the necessity to protect and sustain nature. He maintained that when industrialists engage in nature, the natural world will suffer. Some of the most protections have put in place ways to conservation from capitalism.

Ecology, the interaction of humans with nature, has become one of the most critical challenges of our time. The political divide is clear: some eco-entrepreneurs seek to protect the commons, while others do not see any urgency to change the norms of the industrial age.

What can be done? Scandinavians have the legitimacy to lead and put issues on the table, while many larger states have multiple agendas, yet Sweden, Norway, Denmark, Iceland, and Finland practice with policies that introduce incentives defining the greening of societies.

The 1972 UN Convention on the Environment introduced multilateralism, forging the largest world discussions on ecology. One idea included the adopting of new cabinet posts at the Ministry of the Environment, and the Scandinavians led the way as an example. Yet still, other countries were more reticent to follow suit.

Green societies have the capacity to act decisively and think ahead, to prepare for future generations, important to assessing how and why northern countries pace ahead of the metrics developed by the EPI, created by Columbia University and Yale University which offer a systematic comparison by the strength of data to determine the eco-societal variables to rank their competitiveness.

Typically, the five green societies are likely to be at the top of the list. And all these countries are competing among themselves to be at the top of the Scandinavian list, and it also competes with other leading ecological societies, our green societies.

In 2022, five Scandinavian states listed in order: Denmark (1) Finland (3); Sweden (5); Iceland (10); and Norway, slightly lower.

Consider why the Danes are the leading, above all the states in the EPI.

# Denmark

Denmark's society is distinctive and charming: windmills, green dining, and biking to work, with the leading ecological society in the world according to EPI. The Danes promote clean energy is visible along the coast; pumping rapidly are the blades of the metal windmills developed by the firm Vestas, which they export throughout the world.

Green dining (from field to table) has created a distinctive cuisine using only ingredients that are fresh and local. Carnation is the name of the most popular restaurant throughout Scandinavia—and beyond. While other Nordics also use what is in season, Denmark stands out in global dining and creates a *hygge* or cozy ambiance.

The ecological Danes adopted a green policy adopted to for paid a fee on bottles with an ecological payback. Returned coins deliver all those empty, in a revolving machine. By making the landscape less clean, Denmark developed a way to convince the European Court of Justice (ECJ) that this was fair for all by fewer bottles in the environment.

For mobility, clean trains painted red and white are quick and ecological markings in cars. It helps that the terrain is flat and bikers seem to fly through Copenhagen, for a nonpolluting way to get to work. There is no such race on bikes in the cities of Sweden, Iceland, Finland, or Norway. This is Denmark—ranked number 1 in the world by the EPI.

CHRISTINE INGEBRITSEN

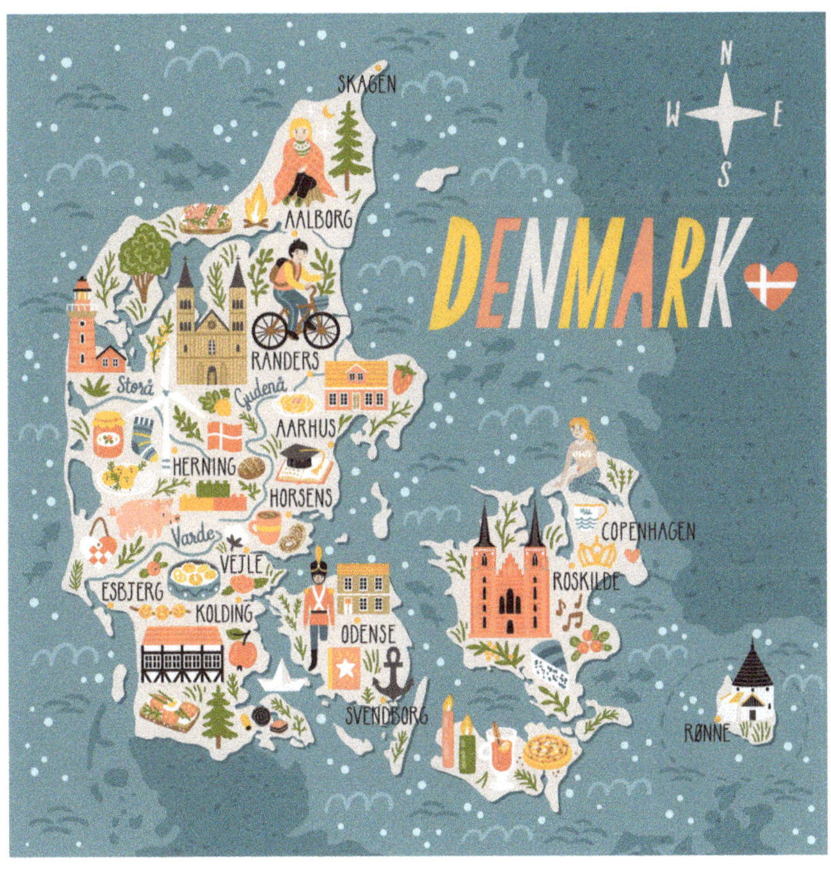

SKAGEN
AALBORG
RANDERS
Storå
Gudenå
AARHUS
HERNING
HORSENS
Varde
VEJLE
ESBJERG
KOLDING
ODENSE
SVENDBORG
DENMARK
N
W
E
S
COPENHAGEN
ROSKILDE
RØNNE

# Finland

Finland's ecology stems from the early timber regulation in the 1800s, the development of a robust tech industry (Nokia cellphone), and a sparse and unique fabrics, glass, and wood using what is best from their society. Conservationism appeared in strict regulation of the government and was the earliest of green societies to set parameters for how to restrict timber.

The most famous aspect of Finnish culture is the *sauna*. Considered a good way to stay healthy, it has given Finns the reputation of being *sisu* (inner strength) as they jump in a cold lake, even when they meet guests from other societies. Throughout the world, Finnish saunas are very popular at home and imported by countries abroad. As the economy diversified to technology and cell phones, Nokia has been the most successful firms in the Nordic area.

Without the hydropower in Norway, the Swedish diversified economy, the absence of Icelandic cod or geothermal energy, and a Danish cycling culture, Finland's education, timber and Nokia sectors, are defining aspects to eco-institutionalism. The Finns had the first ever regulations on timber, leading the way to conservation ahead of the other Nordics. See the image of early timber (birch trees).

While Finland is known for being fierce during the Second World War and trading off timber profits to technology firms such as Nokia, Finland has joined the North Atlantic Treaty Organization (NATO) and will bring its green society and ways as a valued contributor to ecological discussions as well as securing borders. It is ranked by EPI second place as an ecologically minded smaller state with a reputation of a leading educational system and was the first to conserve precious resources of timber.

FINLAND
LAPLAND
SAARISELKA
ROVANIEMI
KUUSAMO
KEMI
OULU
KOKKOLA
NURMES
LIEKSA
VAASA
SAVONLINNA
GULF OF BOTHNIA
TAMPERE
TURKU
ESPOO
HELSINKI
BALTIC SEA
N
W
E
S

# Sweden

Sweden is the largest of the green societies and prides itself on cleaning the water around the Parliament, allowing the revival of fishing in the center of Stockholm. Prominent Swedes are active in their labs (such as Alfred Nobel) and have been outspoken about nature, ecology, and the role of science.

For example, a well-known Swede Svante Arrhenius was working in a lab at the height of industrialization in the 1880s. One of the experiments examined the relationship between polluting industries and the temperature in Sweden. He noted that a rise of 2 degrees coincided with smokey skies. He called this the *greenhouse effect* and connected industrial activity and the warming of Sweden. The term has become common; however, it was rarely connected to Svante Arrhenius.

*Allemansratt* is a more recent development, acknowledging that the Swedish landscape is for everyone. Camping on a farmer's field must only be left the way it once did before.

Like all the green societies, this is a common way to take care of the land, and this is a norm for Swedish camping and hiking. Sweden also imports garbage to burn for energy. Another economic and ecological way to develop partners across borders.

So Swedish!

CHRISTINE INGEBRITSEN

VIKING
SWEDEN
SAREKS NATIONAL PARK
OLD TOWN
LAGOM
UPPSALA
RIDDARKHOLMEN CHURCH
VASA MUSEUM
STOCKHOLM
VADSTENA CASTLE
TOWN HALL
VISBY
GOTEBORG
FIKA
FALSTERBO
CAFFE

# Iceland

Iceland is the land of ice, fire, and geothermal energy. The smallest of the Nordics harness: geothermal energy beneath the earth, and Reykjavik ("smokey bay") melts the snow to easily access on walkways from the warmness of the earth—Hekla, an active volcano.

Iceland protects its local fishing, the cod. The desire by the British Royal Navy sought to take a catch of the Icelandic cod. However, the Iceland fishermen cut the lines of the British nets. Iceland fiercely retreated, with their cod to take home. To conserve the fish, Iceland proposed a fifty-mile area, and today it has been expanded by two hundred miles away from the coast. It was Iceland that pushed forward the two-hundred-mile sovereignty as the global standard. This is often an example of the *power of the weak*, when the bigger country loses access to prime resources, the Icelandic cod.

Traditional handcrafts are also a source of income, which made Lopi wool, unique in style, acquirable through the Internet.

While other societies protect puffins, whaling and horses, Icelanders allow conservation as long-time culinary traditions.

# Norway

Image of skiing is recreational, yet it competes in world markets (Dale, Helly Hansen, and leading Norwegian companies).

Norway has a mixed economy: conservationist, as a petrol-dependent economy. Yet there are many policies and restraints to pump more oil and gas from the continental shelf. Oil and gas were discovered off the coastline and were developed in the 1970s, yet economists were wary of overheating the economy. Hans Henrik Ramm, a politician, sought a limit to petrodollars and restricted the funds to avoid inflation. Norway thereby avoided the *Dutch disease*: a sudden increase in overheating of the economy from the Netherlands sector of the North Sea. Norwegian policymakers resisted pumping too much petroleum out of the continental shelf and avoided inflation.

How can the petrol-dependent Norwegian political economy be a green society? Only Norway encouraged Tesla's competitive pricing and edge: it's a unique way to go green. And ferries developed to lessen pollution are increasingly popular.

In Norway, the Seed Project has also captured the world's eco-diversity by submitting the "starts" to capture and maintain in a vault deep in the earth.

NORWAY
FOR
WINTER
SPORTS
Daily Service B&N LINE Steamers
from NEWCASTLE-ON-TYNE in connection with
NORWEGIAN STATE RAILWAYS.

# NORWAY

NORTHERN
LIGHTS
KAYAKING
CHEESES
CUTTER
TROLLS
BRUNOST
REINDERR
OSLO
VIKING
FJORDS
WILD
SALMON
DRAKKAR
VIKINGS
WOOL SWEATER
SLEDDING

Location
Europe

Capital
Oslo

Area
385,207 km²

Highest Point
Galdhøpiggen

Population
5,402,171

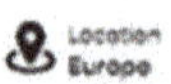

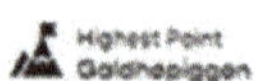

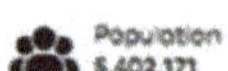

NORWAY
NORWEGIAN SEA
TROMSØ
BODØ
TRONDHEIM
BERGEN
STAVANGER
OSLO
NORTH SEA
N
W E
S

# Scandinavian Global Leaders in the Pursuit of Ecology

Greta Thunberg is a determined young woman leaning against the Swedish Riksdag (Parliament) and refusing to attend school. Her outspoken style and global reach from the United Nations, the European Union, and other multinational organizations have elevated the way ecology, conservation, and entrepreneurship are discussed and debated.

On her first trip to the United States to make a speech at the UN (United Nations), she refused to rely on commercial airlines. Instead, she arrived on a sailboat to make the point that there are other, ecological ways to connect societies in nonpolluting transport.

She was Norway's global voice for conservation, Gro Harlem Brundtland. She served as the Environmental Minister in Norway, a long-time prime minister, and was named to The Elders by Nelson Mandela. The roundtable of former heads of state discusses, among other issues, the state of climate and ways to combat pollution seeking a direct change around the world. The five green societies seek to direct other states to emulate Scandinavia and model the practices for other ways to prepare for the future, and be an upward scale on the Environmental Performance Index (EPI).

# Conclusion

Ecology, the interaction of humans with nature, has become the most critical challenges of our time. There is no one champion for the earth, nor is there protection for human health and safety as ecological conditions change. The political divide is clear: some eco-entrepreneurs seek to protect the commons, while others do not see any urgency to change the norms of the industrial age.

Eco-capitalism captures both the past and how we engage our future. Instead of dwelling on the past, this study seeks to focus on alternative ways capitalists, political leaders, norm entrepreneurs, protectors of nature, and NGOs (non-governmental organizations). Green societies are introducing ways to meet the expectations of the UN Brundtland Committee. Greta Thunberg, and the ecological recommendations of *Our Common Future*, as leaders of the Environmental Performance Index (EPI), Scandinavia continues to bring about changes.

This is the issue of our time.

# Resources

Brundtland, Gro Harlem. *Our Common Future* (UN Report). 1987.

Dauvergne, Peter and Lister, Jane. *Eco-Business: A Big-Brand Takeover of Sustainability.* 2013.

*Environmental Performance Index.* Data from Yale and Columbia. Annual.

Guha, Ramachandra. *Environmentalism: A Global History.* 2020.

Ingebritsen, Christine. "Ecological Institutionalism: Scandinavian and the Greening of Capitalism." 2012.

Ingebritsen, Christine. "Europeanization and Cultural Identity: Two Worlds of Eco-Capitalism." Scandinavian Studies. 2001.

Ingebritsen, Christine. "The Politics of Whaling in Norway and Iceland" (Scandinavian Review). 1997.

Kurlansky, Mark. *Cod.* 1997.

Merlino, Kathryn and Leah Glaser. *Let'sSustain.* 2014

Thunberg, Greta. *No One is Too Small to Make a Difference.* 2018.

Images for each of the five Scandinavian societies, Denmark, Finland, Sweden, Norway, and Iceland.

Leading newspapers, EPI data, Etsy images, and publications.

# About the Author

Fields of Interest
    Ecology and Scandinavia
    Scandinavian Literature and Culture
    Scandinavian Area Studies Norwegian
    Gender, Women, and Sexuality Studies International Studies
    Political Science

Biography
    Ph.D. Cornell University, 1993
    Christine Ingebritsen is a political scientist who teaches and conducts research on the position of small states in international relations. Her work seeks to explain how and why Scandinavian governments (Denmark, Sweden, Norway, Finland, and Iceland) have responded differently to contemporary challenges, from a more globalized international political economy to an integrated Europe. Collectively, Scandinavia seeks to export best practices to international institutions and acts as a *norm entrepreneur* in several important issue areas (the environment, human rights, and security).
    Dr. Ingebritsen is also an adjunct professor of women's studies and an adjunct professor of political science.

Teaching
    • Scandinavia, the EU and Global Climate
    • Scandinavia in World Affairs
    • Environmental Norms in International Politics
    • Modern Scandinavian Politics
    • Women in Scandinavia

See Christine in a *recent video* highlighting the MAAIS (Master of Arts in Applied International Studies) Program at the Jackson School of International Studies.

> - Research
> - Courses Taught
> - Resources and Related Links
> - Affiliations
> - News and Events